Magic Maui Cookbook

Written and Illustrated by
Mama Annie

ISBN 0-9637637-9-2

© copyright 1997 by Cleall Publishing
840 Wainee Street #203
Lahaina, Maui, HI 96761

Andrea Cleall, known to friends and family as Mama Annie, is a long-time, part-time Maui resident. She spends a good part of each year in her Maui kitchen playing with tropical fruits and local spices. Inspired by the multi-ethnic influences in island cuisine, she learned and experimented until she created some very sumptuous recipes. Magic Maui cookbook contains many of her favorites.

Other books by Mama Annie

Island Dancers
Island Adventures
Amazing Sea Creatures
Keli's Magic Stone

Introduction and acknowledgements

Many, many years ago, when I started spending a lot of time in Maui, my friends, who knew my passion for food, would ask me what I ate in Hawaii. I always said "I don't go to Maui to eat". There has always been fresh fruit and fish but good restaurants were few and far between. Boy, has that changed! Now, with the influx of brilliant young chefs from all over the world, Hawaii is not only the paradise it has always been but is also a gastronomic Eden. I don't pretend to have the training or even the creativity of these kitchen geniuses, but I thank them for the inspiration and the influence they've had on my home cooking. I hope you enjoy my cookbook and I encourage you to wander, dreamy-eyed, through ethnic grocery stores saying, "I wonder what this is — wonder what that would taste like"— etc. etc.

I would like to thank my family for all the tasting, my son Sean for his flattering drawing of my kitchen and Claudia Cannon, my distributor, for her constant encouragement.

TABLE OF CONTENTS

Appetizers

Corn and Shrimp Cakes

1 1/4 cup flour

1/3 cup corn flour or corn meal

2 tsp. baking powder

3/4 tsp. salt

1 egg

4 Tbsp. melted butter

1 1/2 cup milk

corn from 1 large cob

1/2 cup bay shrimp

2 Tbsp. minced chives

1/2 tsp. thyme

*Plum sauce or hot sauce

Mix egg, butter and milk. Sift together dry ingredients and add to egg mixture. Fold in corn, shrimp, chives and thyme. Preheat oiled skillet and pour 1/4 cup batter. Cook until bubbles formed on top pop and begin to look dry. Turn over and cook until lightly browned. Serve two cakes to a plate for a first course, with Plum sauce or hot sauce on the side.

Plum sauce is available in most grocery stores in the Asian section.

Serves 4

Chicken Liver Toasts

1 pound chicken livers

2 slices Canadian bacon

3 Tbsp. butter

1/2 tsp. sage

salt and pepper

1/4 cup Guava or Current jelly

1/4 cup red wine

3 slices bread, cut into 4 triangles each

2 Tbsp. butter

Mince Canadian bacon. Cut chicken livers in half and saute 5 minutes in two Tbsp. butter with Canadian bacon, sage and salt and pepper. Saute bread triangles in 1 Tbsp. butter and place on four plates, three per plate. Remove liver mixture from pan and place on top of toast triangles. Keep warm. Add jelly and wine to liver pan and cook 3 minutes. Add remaining Tbsp. butter to pan, swirl into sauce until melted and pour over livers.

Serves 4

Asian Fire Roasted Corn

4 large ears of corn, with husks

1 Tbsp. vegetable oil

1 Tbsp. chili powder

1 1/2 tsp. coarse salt

1 Tbsp. Hoisin sauce*

Soak corn in husks in cold water for 30 minutes. Mix remaining ingredients. Drain corn. Pull back husks carefully so as not to detach from corn. Remove silk. Brush corn with oil mix. Pull husks back over corn and tie at the top with kitchen string or strings pulled from corn husks. Grill 30 minutes on a barbeque or in a hot oven, turning often.

Hoisin sauce is available in the Asian section of most markets.

Serves 4

Alii Caviar Cake

This appetizer is elegant, easy and very pretty. Serve it with crackers or cocktail breads on an attractive platter.

1 8 oz. block cream cheese

1 small jar black caviar

2 lemons

2 hard-boiled eggs

1/4 cup each, finely chopped parsley, chives and celery

Place cheese in center of serving plate and cover the top with caviar. Squeeze one lemon over all. Finely chop boiled eggs. Arrange around edges of cheese block. Arrange chopped greens around eggs. Thinly slice other lemon and overlap slices on top of cheese block. Serve crackers on outer edge of plate or on another plate.

Serves 10 to 12

Malia's Egg Puffs

This recipe can be made bite-size for hors d'oeuvres or a little larger as a luncheon dish to be served with soup or salad.

small or medium cream puff shells

6 hard boiled eggs, chopped small

2 Tbsp. minced parsley

1 Tbsp. minced fresh cilantro

2 green onions, minced

1 tsp. minced fresh ginger

4 Tbsp. mayonnaise

2 Tbsp. chili sauce

1/2 tsp. dry Chinese mustard

Combine eggs, parsley, cilantro, onions and ginger. Combine mayonnaise and chili sauce and fold into egg mixture. Chill. Mound into cream puff shells and serve within an hour.

Serves 4 for lunch
Makes approximately 24 hors d'oeuvres.

Cream Puff Shells

1 cup water

1/2 cup butter, cut in pieces

1/4 tsp. salt

1 cup sifted, all-purpose flour

4 eggs, 3 if very large

Preheat oven to 450 degrees. Pour water into a saucepan and bring to a boil. Add butter and salt and cook until butter melts. Remove from heat and immediately dump in flour and stir vigorously until dough forms ball. Cool slightly. Add eggs, one at a time and beat until mixture is smooth and glossy after each egg is added. Drop mixture by rounded tablespoonsful for big shells and by rounded teaspoons for small ones, on a baking sheet. For large shells bake 15 minutes at 450 degrees, then reduce heat to 350 degrees and bake 20 to 30 minutes longer, or until shells are rigid. For smaller shells, bake 10 minutes at 450 degrees, then reduce heat to 350 degrees and bake 10 to 15 minutes longer.

This recipe is easy to make but it's important to follow directions exactly, adding flour all at once and immediately after mixture leaves heat, and beating eggs thoroughly, one at a time.

Shallot and Mushroom Beignets

This is not a well known island dish but too good to leave out. Serve them with Spam or Portuguese sausage and papaya slices and you'll have an island breakfast. By themselves they're a great appetizer.

1 cup water

1/2 cup butter, cut in pieces

1/4 tsp. salt

1 cup all-purpose flour

4 eggs, 3 if very large

1/2 cup swiss cheese, grated

4 or 5 shallots

8 to 10 mushrooms

1 Tbsp. butter

oil for frying

This is the same dough as is used for cream puffs, but it is deep fried instead of baked. Boil the 1 cup water, add butter and salt until butter melts. Remove from heat and dump in flour, all at once and stir vigorously until flour forms a ball. Cool slightly. Add eggs, one at a time, and beat until smooth and glossy after each egg is added. Chop shallots and mushrooms into small pieces and saute in butter for 2 or 3 minutes. Fold these and grated cheese into batter. Drop mixture by tablespoons into hot oil, 375 degrees, and cook until puffed and golden.

Makes 20 to 24 beignets

Island Ahi Sashimi

1 1/2 pound sashimi-grade ahi

1/2 cup lime juice

1/4 cup finely chopped bell pepper

2 Tbsp. finely chopped cilantro

3 green onions,finely chopped

1/2 cup coconut milk

1 tsp. salt

lettuce leaves

Cut fish in very thin, bite-size slices. Mix salt and lime juice and cover fish. Marinate at least two hours in the refrigerator. Add pepper, cilantro, onion and coconut milk to fish and marinade. Chill slightly and serve over lettuce leaves.

Serves 4 or more

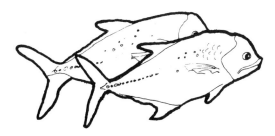

Roasted Stuffed Peppers

1/2 pound feta cheese

2 red bell peppers

2 green bell peppers

2 cloves garlic, minced

1 small onion, finely chopped

2 Tbsp. pine nuts or macadamia nuts, chopped

1 Tbsp. chopped cilantro

Maui salsa (page 36)

Roast peppers according to directions on following page. Cut peppers in half, remove seed and place on a baking sheet. Crumble feta in bowl and add cilantro, onion, garlic and nuts. Mix. If you use pine nuts, toast them in the oven or a small skillet just until brownish, 1 or 2 minutes. They burn easily. Fill pepper halves with this mixture. Broil until bubbly. Put one green and one red pepper half on each of four plates. Surround with salsa and garnish with cilantro sprigs.

Serves 4

To Roast Peppers

Peppers are roasted over direct heat or under a broiler. It is important to keep peppers close to high heat so the skin blackens without over cooking the pepper. For the broiler method, place peppers on baking sheet and place no more than two inches below the heating element. It is necessary to turn the peppers often. When skin is mostly blackened on all sides, remove from heat and put peppers in a paper bag. Close the bag and leave it for ten minutes.

Remove peppers. Peel off charred skin. Now peppers are ready to cut in half or in strips to marinate or stuff or use in any recipe. Before using them, remove the seeds. The method is the same on the grill or barbeque, just remember to keep rack close to heat.

Kona Fried Mozzarella

4 squares mozzarella, 2"x2"x1/2"

1/4 cup Italian breadcrumbs

1/4 cup finely chopped macadamia nuts

1/4 cup milk

3 Tbsp. cooking oil

1/2 cup marinara sauce or pesto*

Mix nuts and breadcrumbs. Dip cheese squares first in milk, then in the nut mixture. Refrigerate one hour or more. Heat oil to medium hot and fry cheese squares, turning to brown on all sides. Drain and serve with marinara sauce or pesto.

* Marinara sauce and pesto are both available in most markets but if you want to make them yourself, I've included recipes on the next page.

Serves 4

Pesto

2 cups fresh basil leaves

2 cloves garlic

3 Tbsp. pine nuts

3/4 cup olive oil

1/2 cup freshly grated Parmesan or Romano cheese

Combine first four ingredients in food processor or blender. Blend until pasty. Add cheese and blend 5 seconds more.

Marinara Sauce

1 small onion, chopped small

2 cloves garlic, minced

1 16 oz. can chopped tomatoes, or

3 large fresh tomatoes, chopped

1/2 tsp. each, basil and oregano

1/4 tsp. fennel seeds (optional)

2 Tbsp. olive oil

1/4 cup red wine or 1 Tbsp. red wine vinegar

salt to taste

Combine all ingredients in a medium saucepan and simmer for 30 minutes, adding water if needed.

Stuffed Lichi Nuts

This is an appealingly different appetizer and also doubles as a lovely, light finger dessert.

1 can litchi nuts, 16 oz.

1 4 oz. package cream cheese

2 or 3 Tbsp. fruit juice or fruit liqueur

1 package macadamia nuts

Combine cream cheese with fruit juice or fruit liqueur or syrup from litchi nuts until the consistency of peanut butter. Drain litchi nuts. Stuff a teaspoon or so of cheese mixture into hollow of nut and press in 1 whole macadamia nut. Add a little more cheese if necessary. Continue until all nuts are filled. Chill.

Soups & Salads

Chicken Coconut Soup

2 skinless chicken breasts

2 cloves garlic, minced

4 cups chicken broth

1 tsp. chopped ginger

8 to 10 mushrooms, chopped

a few drops sesame oil

1 tsp. rice vinegar

1 small (5 oz.) can coconut milk

salt to taste

Cook chicken breasts and garlic in chicken broth for 12 minutes, or until chicken is no longer pink inside. Remove chicken from broth and set aside. Add ginger, mushrooms, sesame oil and vinegar to broth and cook 5 minutes. Meanwhile chop chicken into bite-size pieces. Now return chicken to broth with coconut milk. Cook 1 minute to heat and add salt to taste.

Serves 4

Cream of Broccoli Soup with Gorgonzola

1 large onion

1 clove garlic

1 bunch broccoli, approximately 1 lb.

2 Tbsp. butter

2 cups chicken broth

1 bay leaf

1/2 tsp. dried thyme

3 Tbsp. Gorgonzola cheese

1 cup milk or half and half

salt to taste

almonds or macadamia nuts

Coarsely chop vegetables. Melt butter in saucepan and saute onion and garlic for 3 minutes, stirring to prevent browning. Add broccoli, chicken broth and spices. Cook 15 minutes, or until vegetables are tender. Remove from heat and cool. Put soup, in batches, in blender, until all is blended. Return soup to saucepan and heat. Stir in cheese until it melts. Add milk or cream and cook just until heated through. Add salt, if needed. Chop nuts and sprinkle on soup just before serving.

Serves 4 or 6
as a first course

Fine Fish Chowder

1/2 cup finely diced ham or Canadian bacon

cooking oil or spray

1 large onion, chopped

4 small potatoes, chopped

1 1/2 cups white fish, cod, mahi mahi etc.

1 3/4 cup chicken broth

1 bay leaf

1/2 tsp. each, thyme and marjoram

1 can creamed corn

1 cup milk or half and half

salt and pepper to taste

Saute ham in a little cooking oil or spray 5 minutes or so. Add onions and potatoes and cook 5 minutes more, stirring frequently. Add chicken broth and spices. Cook 5 minutes until vegetables are tender. Add fish and cook 2 to 3 minutes. Add corn and milk and cook just until heated. Add salt and pepper to taste.

Serves 6

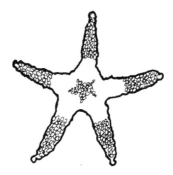

Tutu's Tortilla Soup

2 1/2 cups chicken broth

1 15 oz. can chopped tomatoes

1 onion, chopped small

2 cloves garlic, minced

1 small green pepper, chopped small

corn off 2 cobs

1 medium zucchini, chopped

1 Tbsp. chopped cilantro

1 tsp. chili powder

1/2 tsp. cumin

6 corn tortillas

cooking oil

sour cream

In a large saucepan combine chicken broth, tomatoes, onion, garlic, green pepper, corn and spices. Simmer on low heat for 20 minutes. Add zucchini and cilantro and cook 5 minutes more. Meanwhile cut tortillas in wedges and fry in cooking oil until crisp. Drain. Put soup in bowls. Stir in tortilla wedges and top with a dab of sour cream.

Serves 4

Vitamin A Soup

This soup is good hot or chilled. For a special dinner, substitute cream or half and half for the milk, and serve a lemon slice and a sprig of parsley on top. And maybe think up a fancier name.

1 onion, chopped

1/2 pound carrots, chopped

1 small yam, peeled and chopped

1 cup pumpkin

2 cups chicken broth

1 sage leaf or 1/2 tsp. dried sage

1 bay leaf

1/2 tsp. cumin

1 1/2 cup milk

juice of 1/2 lemon

Cook first 8 ingredients over medium heat until vegetables are tender, about 15 minutes. Remove from heat, cool and puree in blender. Return to pan and add lemon juice, salt to taste and milk. Soup should be a little thick. Add more or less milk to attain desired thickness.

Serves 4 to 6

Avocado Soup with Bay Shrimp

This is light soup, good hot or chilled, and a perfect first course for a formal meal.

1 leek, sliced

1 onion, chopped

1 medium potato, chopped

1 bay leaf

1 sage leaf or a pinch of dried sage

2 cups chicken broth

1 large ripe avocado

1 cup milk or half and half

1/2 cup bay shrimp

Heat chicken broth in a large saucepan. Add leek, onion, potato, bay leaf and sage and cook 20 minutes until vegetables are tender. Cool and blend, in batches, in food processor or blender. Return to saucepan. Stir in mashed avocado and milk. Heat or chill. Salt to taste. Divide among 4 bowls and top with shrimp.

Serves 4

Maui Onion Soup

This soup is very simple and very good.

4 large or 6 small Maui onions

1 tsp. sugar

2 cups chicken broth

salt and pepper

1 Tbsp. brandy or sherry

a good baguette

Peel and slice onions very thin. Put onions and sugar in a heavy saucepan and cook over very low heat for 30 to 40 minutes, stirring frequently, until well browned and glazed. Add the 2 broths. Cook on low heat another 30 minutes. Add brandy or sherry and salt and pepper to taste. Cut 4 slices 3/4 inch thick, from the baguette and toast them. Divide the soup among 4 oven-proof bowls and place 1 piece of toast on each. Top with a slice of cheese and broil until cheese is bubbly.

Serves 4

Pele's Soup

It'll warm you up.

4 dried shitake mushrooms

3 cups chicken broth

1 Tbsp. soy sauce

1/2 cup bamboo shoots

1/4 pound cooked pork, cut in strips

1 cake tofu

2 Tbsp. lemon juice

1/4 tsp. white pepper

2 Tbsp. cornstarch dissolved in 3 Tbsp. cold water

1 egg, slightly beaten

2 tsp. sesame oil

Soak mushrooms in water 15 minutes or until tender. Cut out stem and cut mushrooms in strips. Combine broth, soy sauce, mushrooms, bamboo shoots and pork in saucepan and boil 3 minutes. Add tofu, lemon juice and pepper, heat to boil and turn down to simmer. Stir in cornstarch mixture to thicken. Pour in egg and stir 10 seconds. Add sesame oil and remove from heat. Garnish with chopped green onion.

Serves 4

Pupu Potato Salad

2 medium red onions, sliced very thin

8 medium red potatoes, cooked and sliced thin

6 slices bacon, fried crisp

4 oranges, peeled and sliced thin

2 cups mixed greens

4 oz. blue cheese

large lettuce leaves

tangy vinaigrette

Line each of four plates with large lettuce leaves. Divide mixed greens among four plates, arranging them on top of large leaves. Overlap potatoes, onions and orange slices on lettuce mix. Crumble bacon and blue cheese over that and top with vinaigrette.

Tangy Vinaigrette Dressing

1/2 cup salad oil

3 Tbsp. balsamic vinegar

1 tsp. dijon mustard

1 tsp. honey

salt and pepper to taste

Combine all ingredients and blend well.

Pear Pecan Salad

This salad is simple and elegant, wonderful between courses.

1 large head butter lettuce

2 ripe pears, peeled

1/2 cup whole pecans

1/4 pure maple syrup

dressing (recipe follows)

Wash and dry lettuce and tear into bite-size pieces. Arrange on four salad plates. Cut peeled pears into lengthwise wedges. Arrange on lettuce. Put syrup in a bowl and stir the pecans in the syrup. Remove pecans to a baking sheet and bake for 10 minutes at 375 degrees. Cool and add to salad. Top with dressing.

Dressing

1/2 cup plain yogurt

2 Tbsp. olive oil

2 Tbsp. pure maple syrup

Combine all ingredients.

Serves 4

Sweet Potato Salad

4 cups cooked sweet potato, peeled and cubed
1/2 cup green onion, chopped small
1/4 cup chopped daikon radish
1/4 cup chopped cilantro
1/2 cup chopped pistachios or macadamia nuts
dressing
(recipe follows)

Combine all ingredients and toss gently with dressing.

Dressing

6 Tbsp. salad oil
2 Tbsp. white wine vinegar
2 Tbsp. orange juice
1 tsp. honey
salt to taste

Blend all ingredients and salt to your own taste.

Serves 6

Tropical Spinach Salad

1 bunch well cleaned spinach

3 slices Canadian bacon

2 Tbsp. coarsely chopped macadamia nuts

2 Tbsp. lemon juice

3 Tbsp. olive oil

3 Tbsp. mango chutney

salt and pepper

Dry spinach and tear into bite-size pieces. Mince Canadian bacon and saute in one Tbsp. olive oil. Remove bacon and add to pan 2 more Tbsp. olive oil and mango chutney. Heat and set aside. Put spinach in salad bowl, sprinkle lemon over spinach and toss. Add macadamia nuts and bacon. Just before serving, add warm oil mixture and toss. Add salt and pepper to taste.

Serves 4

Thai Salad

This is certainly the most unusual salad I've ever had. It's based on a Thai recipe called "galloping horses". Don't be afraid of it. It's absolutely delicious.

4 navel oranges, peeled, sliced thin, slices cut in half

1 tsp. salad oil or spray

1 large garlic clove, minced

1/4 pound mild sausage

2 Tbsp. finely chopped macadamia nuts

1 tsp. sugar

1 Tbsp. soy sauce

1 Tbsp. water

salt and pepper

mint leaves

Saute sausage and garlic in oil, breaking sausage into very small pieces. When sausage is cooked add nuts, soy sauce, sugar and water. Salt and pepper to taste. Arrange orange halves and mint leaves on a salad plate and sprinkle warm sausage mix over this. Serve immediately.

Serves 4

No Ka Oi Pork Salad

This is a great way to use leftover pork roast. The miso based dressing compliments the pork nicely and is very low in fat.

1/2 pound cooked pork loin, sliced thin

2 Maui onions sliced thin

4 tomatoes, sliced

3 cups assorted lettuce greens

2 Tbsp. miso*

1 Tbsp. salad oil

1 Tbsp. rice vinegar

1/4 tsp. sesame oil

1 tsp. honey

2 Tbsp. water

salt, if needed

Make dressing. Mix miso, salad oil, sesame oil, vinegar and honey. Thin with water if it's too thick and add salt if needed. Toss lettuce with 2/3 of the dressing. Divide lettuce among 4 plates and arrange pork, onions and tomatoes on lettuce. Drizzle remaining salad dressing over all. Serve with a crusty french bread.

* Miso is a soybean paste, available in Asian markets. It makes a wonderful soup base as those of you who frequent sushi bars know. It comes in white and red. I prefer the white.

Serves 4

Stuffed Cucumber Salad

4 cucumbers

2 medium tomatoes, chopped 1/4 inch

4 green onions, chopped

1 small can crushed pineapple, drained

green ginger mayonnaise (recipe follows)

1/4 cup chopped macadamia nuts

Peel cucumbers and cut in half lengthwise. Simmer in water to cover for 2 minutes. Cool and scoop out centers with seeds. Mix together tomatoes, onions and pineapple with green ginger mayonnaise. Mound in hollows of cucumbers and sprinkle top with nuts.

Green Ginger Mayonnaise

1/4 cup combined parsley and cilantro leaves

1/4 tsp chopped ginger

1 Tbsp. lemon juice

1 cup mayonnaise (I use low-fat)

Combine parsley, cilantro, ginger and lemon juice in blender. Blend well. Add a little of the mayonnaise if you haven't enough liquid. Fold green mix into mayonnaise.

Serves 4 generously

Light Meals

Tropical Burritos

2 pounds flank steak

1/4 cup olive oil

1/4 cup white wine vinegar

3 cloves garlic, chopped

1/2 tsp. each, salt and oregano

1/8 tsp. pepper

2 avocados, cubed

1 cup diced pineapple

flour tortillas

Marinate steaks at least six hours in mixture of olive oil, vinegar, garlic, oregano, salt and pepper. Barbeque steak and slice into thin strips. Heat tortillas in oven. Fill tortilla with steak strips, avocado and pineapple. Top with salsa.

Serves 4 to 6

Maui Salsa

3 large Maui tomatoes

2 Maui onions

1 4oz. can diced jalapeno peppers

1 Tbsp. oil

1 Tbsp. vinegar

2 Tbsp. chopped cilantro

1/2 tsp. each, oregano and chili powder

salt and pepper to taste

Chop tomatoes into 1/2 inch pieces, and onions into 1/4 inch pieces. Combine both with the remaining ingredients and serve on Tropical Burritos, or anything else.

Pan Pacific Chicken Salad

3 boneless, skinless chicken breasts.

1/2 cup orange juice

1 large garlic clove, minced

1 tsp. fresh ginger, minced

1 Tbsp. vegetable oil

1 Tbsp. soy sauce

1/2 cup chicken broth

6 Tbsp. peanut butter

3 Tbsp. mango chutney

1 package fettuccine

2 cups bean sprouts

salad greens

Cut chicken breasts in four or five slices lengthwise. Combine orange juice, garlic, ginger, oil and soy sauce. Marinate chicken in this mixture for one hour or more. Remove chicken and place on a broiling pan. Reserve marinade. Combine marinade in saucepan with chicken broth, peanut butter,and mango chutney. Simmer until smooth, two or three minutes. Broil chicken strips five minutes, or until done. Cook pasta according to package directions and add bean sprouts to pasta for the last minute of cooking. Drain pasta and sprouts and toss to combine. Arrange salad greens around edge of four plates. Put pasta mix in center, with chicken strips on top. Pour sauce over all and serve.

Serves 4

Crabcakes with
Mango Remoulade Sauce

2 Tbsp. butter

2 Tbsp. green onion, chopped small

1/2 cup breadcrumbs

1 egg, beaten

1/2 cup cream or buttermilk

2 cups flaked crabmeat

2 tsp. Dijon mustard

flour or cornmeal

Melt butter in large skillet. Saute green onions and breadcrumbs over medium heat, stirring for two minutes. Add remaining ingredients and chill. Form into four patties, dust with flour or cornmeal and fry on medium heat 2 or 3 minutes per side. Serve with mango remoulade sauce.

sauce (on next page)

Mango Remoulade Sauce

3/4 cup mayonnaise

1 Tbsp. capers

1 tsp. horseradish

1/2 tsp. dried tarragon

1 tsp. finely chopped parsley

2 mangos

a dash or two of tabasco sauce

Combine the first five ingredients. Add tabasco sauce to desired hotness. Peel mangos thoroughly, as the peel causes an allergic reaction in some people. Cut four slices from the mangos and chop the rest into small pieces. Add the pieces to the sauce. Arrange the sauce on two or four plates and top with the crabcakes. Add a slice of mango to each plate and garnish with parsley sprigs.

Serves 2 or 4

Fresh Maui Tomato Pasta

3 Tbsp. olive oil

2 shallots

1 large clove garlic, chopped

3 anchovy filets

2 cups chopped, fresh, very ripe tomatoes

1/2 cup water

2 Tbsp. tomato paste

1 Tbsp. red wine vinegar

1 Tbsp. fresh or 1 tsp. dried, basil

1 Tbsp. fresh or 1 tsp. dried, oregano

10 or 12 oil-cured black olives

pasta

In a saucepan or skillet combine olive oil, shallots, garlic and anchovies until they are blended. Add remaining ingredients except pasta and cook over low heat for another twenty minutes. Serve over cooked pasta. Grated Romano cheese may be sprinkled on top if you like. This is a light meal, served with bread and salad, for four or a generous meal for two.

Makawao Meatballs

1 pound ground beef

1/2 pound pork sausage

2 cloves garlic, minced

1/4 cup finely chopped parsley

1/2 cup breadcrumbs

2 eggs

dash of white wine

1 tsp. Italian herbs

1/2 tsp. salt

oil for cooking

1 cup beef broth

2 heaping Tbsp. tomato paste

1/2 cup chopped pineapple with juice

Mix first nine ingredients to a smooth paste. Form into small balls and brown well, in batches. Add beef broth, tomato paste and pineapple. Simmer, covered, on low heat for 1/2 hour. Serve with noodles or as an appetizer.

Serves 4

Shrimp Picante

1 pound jumbo shrimp

1 Tbsp. butter

1 Tbsp. olive oil

1 large garlic clove

sherry

2 Tbsp. chopped parsley

2 Tbsp. chopped mint

2 Tbsp. tomato paste

1/2 tsp. hot chili paste or hot chili oil

Butterfly the shrimp (see next page). Melt butter with oil in saute pan. Peel garlic and slice clove in half lengthwise. Swirl both halves in butter and oil to flavor it. Add shrimp and cover with a flat lid to prevent shrimp from curling too much. Cook 2 or 3 minutes over medium heat, until shrimp are pink. Remove shrimp, add tomato paste, a dash or two of sherry, and a little water. Cook 1 minute to reduce liquid. Add chili oil slowly to desired hotness. Add parsley and mint and return shrimp to pan until just heated. Serve as an appetizer or with rice or pasta.

Serves 4

To Butterfly Shrimp

Remove legs from shrimp. Shell and tail can be removed or left on. Either way, slit shrimp down outside curve (or back), without cutting all the way through. Remove vein. Shrimp can now be flattened into a butterfly shape. Shell and tail are often left on for scampi style shrimp. They look attractive and add flavor to the sauce.

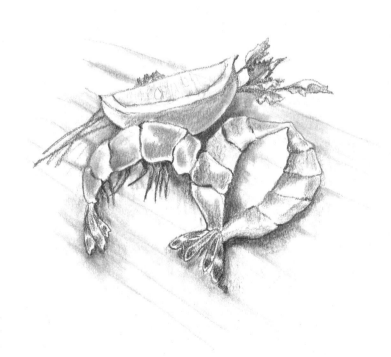

Fishburgers on Sourdough

1 1/2 pounds fresh fish, ahi, mahi-mahi, or ono

1 loaf sourdough bread

8 slices bacon

8 slices jack cheese

8 slices onion

2 tomatoes, sliced

Green ginger mayonnaise

Cut fish in slices 1/2 inch thick. Grill or saute. Cook bacon until crisp, remove, drain fat and saute onions in same pan. Cut bread in 8 slices and spread each with green ginger mayonnaise. Assemble each sandwich starting with one slice bread, then fish, cheese, bacon, onion, tomato and other slice bread. Serve with french fries or fresh fruit.

Serves 4

Green Ginger Mayonnaise

1 cup low-fat mayonnaise

1 Tbsp. lemon juice

1/2 tsp. chopped ginger

1/4 cup combined fresh parsley and mint leaves, chopped

Combine lemon juice, ginger, parsley and mint in blender. Blend until mixed. Mix with mayonnaise.

Stuffed Eggplant

2 large eggplants

1 large onion

3 cloves garlic

3 Tbsp. olive oil

1 pound mushrooms, coarsely chopped

3 Tbsp. fresh basil, chopped

1/4 cup parsley, chopped

1 tsp. dried oregano

1/2 tsp. or more salt

1/2 pound mozzarella or strong feta*

Cut eggplants in half and carefully remove pulp, leaving shells intact. Chop pulp coarsely and salt shells and pulp. Leave sit for an hour or so. Drain. This process removes excess moisture from the eggplant, improving it's texture. In large skillet, saute onion and garlic in olive oil. When vegetables are soft, add chopped eggplant and mushrooms, basil, parsley, oregano and salt to taste. Saute a few minutes. Stir in grated mozzarella or crumbled feta. Stir to combine and mound mixture into the reserved shells. Place on cookie sheet and bake at 325 degrees for thirty minutes. Grated parmesan or romano can be sprinkled on top, but is not necessary.

I like a strong French or Bulgarian feta in this dish, but for a milder, creamier flavor, mozzarella is very good.

Serves 4

Seafood Tamales

These take a little time but the process is fun and the result is fabulous.

Masa

1 package corn husks, soaked 5 minutes and rinsed well

2 cups masa harina (corn flour, not corn meal)

2 cups chicken broth

1/3 cup oil, may be part butter

1/4 tsp. salt

Combine all ingredients to form a soft dough, adding more chicken broth if necessary if not spreadable.

Filling

1 tsp. butter

1/2 cup chopped onion

1 clove garlic, chopped

1 Tbsp. minced lemon grass or 1 tsp. grated lemon rind

1/2 pound firm fish

1 pound shrimp, shelled

salt and pepper

Lightly steam fish and shrimp. Melt butter in skillet and saute onion, garlic and lemon grass for 2 or 3 minutes. Combine with fish and shrimp.

Sauce (on next page)

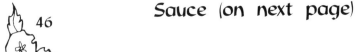

Sauce

2 cups chicken broth

3 rounded Tbsp. corn starch

2 Tbsp. curry paste

2 Tbsp. peanut butter

3/4 cup coconut milk

Dissolve corn starch in cold chicken broth. Heat, stirring until thickened slightly. Add curry paste and peanut butter. Stir until combined. Add coconut milk and heat through. Makes 1 to 1 1/2 dozen. See next page for directions in forming tamales.

Forming and Cooking Tamales

Spread cleaned husks on your work surface. You may need 2 husks if they're small. Stick them together with a little masa dough to form a loose rectangle. Spread a small amount of dough (2 or 3 Tbsp.) in the middle of the husks and spread to form a rectangle about 3 by 4 inches. This need be nowhere near this exact, It's just a general picture. Now place 1 Tbsp. fish mixture in center and fold edges of husk toward center covering fish with the dough. You can add a little dough on top of fish if necessary. You now fold husk into a little package folding all ends to the same side. Place fold side down in a steam pan. This sounds vague but you get the knack quickly once you start. You can also roll them and tie the ends like a firecracker, making sure the fish is surrounded by dough. Pile them one on top of another, folded side down. Steam over water for an hour. When done you may remove them from the husks or serve them in the husks and allow your guests to remove them. Either way serve them on a bed of sauce, 2 or 3 to a plate.

Shopping Tips

Masa harina is the corn flour used to make tortillas. Masa is also the name used for the tamale dough. Many large grocery stores routinely stock masa harina. Your health food store should also have it. The same is true of the corn husks but if you can't find them, wait until corn is in season. The fresh green husks not only work wonderfully but are considered a special treat due to enhanced flavor.

Macadamia Nut Fried Rice

2 cups long grain rice

1/2 cup macadamia nuts

2 large eggs

1/4 pound bulk sausage

6 green onions, finely chopped

1 Tbsp. fresh ginger, finely chopped

2 Tbsp. sherry or saki

3 Tbsp. soy sauce

salt if needed

3 Tbsp. vegetable oil

1 head butter lettuce

Rinse rice in cold water until water is clear. Cook rice in 4 cups water for 12 minutes, without lifting lid. Remove from heat and let stand five minutes. Spread rice on baking sheet and chill. Heat wok to medium-high. Add 1/2 tablespoon oil and the eggs. Cook, stirring to break eggs into small pieces. Transfer eggs to plate. Add 1/2 tablespoon oil to pan with sausage and cook quickly, breaking sausage into small pieces. Transfer to plate. Add nuts. Cook just until they begin to brown and transfer to plate. Add remaining oil along with ginger and onion. Stir fry for two minutes. Add cold rice and stir until heated. Add sherry, soy sauce, salt and nuts and heat through. Stir in eggs and sausage. Spoon rice into a lettuce leaf and eat like a taco.

Serves 4

Fish Tacos

1 pound fish

3 cups shredded cabbage

1 cup shredded red cabbage

juice of 1 lime

2 Tbsp. rice vinegar

1/3 cup vegetable oil

1/4 cup chopped cilantro

salsa verde

corn tortillas

Make coleslaw. Combine cabbages and cilantro. Mix oil, vinegar and lime. Mix with cabbage mix and salt and pepper to taste. Grill or steam fish. Fry tortillas for 10 seconds, turn, add a few chunks of fish and fold to form tacos. Fry until crispy. (Lower-fat tacos may be made by simply warming tortillas in oven, rather than frying.) When cooked, drain tacos and fill each with a few teaspoons of coleslaw. Top with salsa verde. Salsa verde is available in most stores or you can make your own.

Serves 4

Salsa Verde

5 or 6 tomatillos

1 small onion, chopped

2 cloves garlic, chopped

3 fresh jalapenos or 1 4 oz. can
jalapeno peppers, chopped

1 Tbsp. chopped cilantro

1/2 tsp. oregano

Tabasco sauce

salt and pepper

Prepare tomatillos. Remove husks, simmer 10 minutes,and chop.
Add next 5 ingredients. Taste. Add salt and pepper to taste and
tabasco if you want it hotter.

Tomatillos

Not a green tomato, but a member of the gooseberry family, the
tomatillo is important in Mexican cooking. The papery husk is
removed and it is simmered in water for 10 minutes or so. After
cooking, it is chopped or pureed for use in salsas, stews, soups,
etc. The popular salsa verde, or green sauce, is made of onion,
garlic, tomatillos and chiles.

the
Spice
RACK

MAMA'
ANNIE'S fridge

the cupboard of Secret ingredients

the stove ♪♪.

the Receptacle of Rejected ideas

Meat Dishes

Glazed Ham

When my favorite taster tasted Magic Maui sauce, he said, "Mmmmm! This would be good on ham." He's my favorite because he likes everything.

1 country-style ham
1 cup Magic Maui sauce
cloves

Soak ham for 24 hours in cold water, changing water several times. Scrub under cold running water and pat dry. Bake ham, uncovered, 20 to 25 minutes per pound, or until it reaches 160 degrees on a meat thermometer. When ham is done, remove rind with a knife or kitchen shears. Score fat diagonally and stud corners with cloves. Spread Magic Maui sauce over fat and bake 15 minutes more. Serve with more sauce on the side. In warm weather, ham is nice served with sweet potato salad.

Serves multitudes

Magic Maui Sauce

1 cup onion, chopped fine

1 large clove garlic, minced

2 cups fruit puree, mango and apricot or peach

1/2 cup crushed pineapple

1/2 cup tomato sauce

5 Tbsp. cider vinegar

1 tsp. molasses

1 Tbsp. mild California chili powder

1 tsp. hot chili powder

1/2 tsp. salt

1/2 tsp. cumin

2 Tbsp. pomegranate paste* or Asian plum sauce

1 tsp. dry mustard

Puree fruit in blender. Combine fruit with all other ingredients in saucepan and simmer on low heat for 30 minutes. This recipe makes almost 4 cups but it is delicious on rice, chicken, fish or omelets as well. It is also a main ingredient in Magic Maui burgers.

Pomegranate paste is available at middle eastern markets.

Makes 3 1/2 cups

Upcountry Ribs with Roasted Vegetables

3 to 4 pounds country-style ribs

1/2 cup barbeque sauce

8 small or 6 large red potatoes

2 medium Maui onions, sliced
1/2 inch thick

8 carrots, sliced on bias, 1/2 inch thick

3 Tbsp. olive oil

1 Tbsp. balsamic vinegar

1 tsp. each, basil and oregano

salt and pepper

Precook ribs for 10 minutes in microwave or 30 in the oven. Brush with barbeque sauce and grill or roast in oven 30 minutes more at 350 degrees. Cut small potatoes in half, large in 3 or 4 pieces. Mix oil, vinegar, spices and salt and pepper in baking dish approximately 9"x11"x2". Add all vegetables and toss to coat with oil mixture. Roast, uncovered, at 350 degrees for 60 minutes, or until tender. Turn vegetables occasionally.

Serves 4

Braised Pork with Ginger Mango

This is simple and fast to prepare yet gets rave notices.

2 1/2 pounds boneless pork loin

salt and freshly ground pepper

2 Tbsp. oil

2 onions, sliced

2 cups chicken broth

4 slices fresh ginger

1/2 tsp. coriander

2 Tbsp. honey or mango chutney

8 slices mango

Sprinkle meat with salt and pepper. Brown well on all sides in a Dutch oven. Remove pork to a plate and brown onion rings in same pan. Return pork and any juices on plate to pan. Add chicken broth, ginger and coriander. Cover and simmer 1 1/2 hours or until 150 degrees on a meat thermometer. Turn pork occasionally and add water if necessary. When cooked add honey or chutney and simmer 5 minutes more. Remove pork and slice 1/2 inch thick. Add more salt and pepper to sauce in pan if needed. Serve sauce over pork with mango slices on the side.

Serves 4 to 6

Stuffed Pork Chops

4 large rib pork chops, cut 3/4 to 1 inch thick

3/4 cup bread crumbs

1/4 cup chopped water chestnuts

1/4 cup chopped macadamia nuts

1/4 cup chopped green onions

1/4 tsp. salt

3/4 cup chicken broth

1/3 cup fruit juice, orange, apple, passion fruit or a

combination would work

3 Tbsp. teriyaki sauce

1 Tbsp. rice vinegar

Cut a pocket in each of the pork chops. Mix well, the breadcrumbs, water chestnuts, macadamia nuts, green onions and salt. Moisten with 1 Tbsp. of the broth. Fill pockets with this mixture and close with a skewer or a toothpick. Brown chops in oiled skillet. Mix remaining broth with fruit juice, teriyaki sauce and vinegar and pour into skillet with pork chops. Cover and simmer 45 minutes on low heat.

Serves 4

Turkey Cutlets with Litchi Nuts

I first invented this recipe when I found myself with a can of kumquats. It's really delicious and seems equally good with litchis, kumquats or cherries, so use what you like best.

8 turkey cutlets

2 small onions, cut in narrow wedges

1 clove garlic, minced

1 Tbsp. each, olive oil and butter

1 cup litchi nuts

1/2 cup juice from can of litchi nuts

1 tsp. dijon mustard

1/4 tsp. salt

1/4 cup sour cream

1 Tbsp. flour

green fettuccine

butter

In large skillet, saute onions and garlic in 1 Tbsp. each, olive oil and butter for 3 minutes. Push aside and add cutlets. Brown slightly and add litchis and juice. Simmer 5 minutes . Remove cutlets and keep warm. Mix flour with sour cream and add to pan with dijon and salt. Cook 3 minutes. Return cutlets to pan. Cook fettuccine and toss with butter. Serve cutlets and sauce over fettuccine.

Serves 4

Catamaran Cassoulet

So named because this is a hearty dish well-suited to the hunger produced by a day of sailing. It can also be made ahead and served on board!

1 pound small white beans
1 tsp. salt
1 large onion, studded with two whole cloves
2 cloves garlic, minced
2 carrots
1 bay leaf
1 tsp. thyme
2 strips bacon, chopped
1 pound lean pork, cut in 1 inch cubes
6 chicken thighs
3 Portuguese sausages, sliced 1 inch thick
1 cup chopped onion
1/2 cup chopped celery
1 8 oz. can tomato sauce
1 cup white wine

Soak beans in water to cover overnight. Change water. Add salt, onion with cloves, garlic, carrots, spices and bacon to water and simmer 1 hour. Brown pork and chicken in oiled skillet and add to beans. Saute onion and celery in same skillet for 3 or 4 minutes. Add wine and tomato sauce. Add this mixture and sausages to beans and simmer 1 hour. Add water if needed. Transfer to large casserole and bake, uncovered at 350 degrees for 30 minutes. Serve in scooped out kaiser rolls.

Serves 6

Tropical Couscous

2 pounds lamb shoulder, cut into 1 inch cubes

2 onions, cut in thin wedges

3 Tbsp. flour

3 Tbsp. oil

2 Tbsp. tomato paste

1/2 cup red wine

1/4 cup tart fruit jelly, like currant, cherry or plum

1 tsp. fresh ginger, minced

1 Tsp. apple cider vinegar

1 cup fresh peas

1 cup cooked garbanzo beans

1 Tbsp. chopped parsley

1 mango, peeled and cut in chunks

1 package couscous

chopped peanuts

Dust meat with flour and brown with onions in oil in a heavy skillet. Add 5 cups water, tomato paste, wine, jelly, ginger and vinegar. Cover and simmer 1 to 1 1/2 hours, until meat is tender. Add peas and garbanzo beans and simmer 15 minutes more. Cook couscous according to package directions, or if you buy bulk, steam over boiling water for 15 minutes. Stir mango into meat mixture and serve over couscous with nuts and parsley sprinkled on top.

Serves 4 to 6

Grilled Lime and Ginger Chicken with Spicy Greens

2 frying chickens, cut in half or sections

1/2 cup vegetable oil

1/2 cup lime juice

2 Tbsp. finely chopped onion

1 large clove garlic, minced

1 tsp. salt

Combine oil, lime juice, onion, garlic and salt. Marinate chicken in mixture for several hours. Chicken may be barbecued or broiled slowly 6 inches from heat. Halves will take an hour, turning and basting with marinade often, Smaller pieces will take 30 to 40 minutes. Serve with Spicy greens and rice if you wish.

Serves 4 to 6

64

Spicy Greens

1 small head cabbage, shredded

1 head chard, bok choy or kale, shredded

4 green onions, chopped

1 Tbsp. oil

1 Tbsp. miso paste*

4 Tbsp. water

1/2 tsp. sesame oil

1/4 to 1/2 tsp. chili garlic sauce*

salt to taste

1 Tbsp. toasted sesame seeds

Stir fry greens and onion in 1 Tbsp. oil 3 to 4 minutes until limp. Mix the rest of the ingredients and stir into greens. Cook on low heat 5 minutes more. Toast sesame seeds in a pan in the oven or in a dry skillet. Watch them closely, they burn easily. Sprinkle them over greens.

Miso paste and chili garlic sauce are available in Asian markets.

Serves 4 to 6

Stuffed Chicken Breasts

4 chicken breasts, boneless and skinless

4 bacon slices

1 bunch collard greens, kale or chard

2 cloves garlic, minced

4 ounces feta cheese

1 1/2 cups chicken broth

1/2 cup fruit nectar

milk

Italian breadcrumbs

1 Tbsp. each, olive oil and butter

1 rounded Tbsp. cornstarch

Fry bacon crisp. Drain fat, but do not wash pan. Chop greens small. Add with garlic to bacon pan and stir fry until wilted. Dust chicken breasts with flour and pound with kitchen mallet to flatten. Spread each breast with 2 Tbsp. greens, 1 crumbled sliced bacon and 1 Tbsp. crumbled feta. Roll breasts and tie or secure with toothpicks. Dip into milk and then breadcrumbs. Refrigerate for 30 minutes. Brown chicken breasts in oil and butter. Add chicken broth when browned. Simmer on low heat 10 to 15 minutes, or until cooked through. Mix fruit nectar with cornstarch and add to pan, stirring to heat and thicken. Serve with polenta.

Serves 4

Polenta

Polenta is a wonderful alternative to rice, pasta or potatoes. It can be served as the starch with any meat. It can be served covered in marinara sauce or you can form it into patties and fry it.

1 cup cornmeal

1 tsp. salt

5 cups water

1/2 cup fresh parmesan or romano cheese, grated

butter and paprika (optional)

Combine in a bowl, the cornmeal, 1 cup water and the salt. Boil 4 cups water in the top of a double boiler and place over boiling water in the bottom of the double boiler. Slowly stir cornmeal mixture into the 4 cups boiling water. Cook, stirring constantly over high heat until mixture boils. Reduce heat, cover and steam for 15 minutes. Add cheese and steam another 15 minutes. Mound on plate and dot with butter and sprinkle with paprika. You can also buy a packaged polenta mix which is easier and faster to cook.

Serves 4

Lanui Chicken

Lanui means holiday and this is a great holiday dish. It's scrumptious, establishes, without a doubt, your genius in the kitchen and it's easy. Double the recipe for a crowd.

1 large chicken fryer, cut up

1 Tbsp. oil

1/3 cup soy sauce

1/3 cup brown sugar

1/4 cup sherry

1/2 cup water

1/4 cup chopped green onion

3 garlic cloves, minced

1/2 to 1 tsp. dried red pepper flakes,
taste for hotness

1 tsp. minced lemon grass
(fresh ginger can be substituted)

1 tsp. sesame oil

1 heaping Tbsp. hoisin sauce

2 Tbsp. toasted sesame seeds

optional fruit

Wash and dry chicken and brown in oil. Toast sesame seeds in oven or in a dry skillet. Watch them closely, they burn easily. Set aside. Combine remaining ingredients. Pour over chicken and simmer, covered, 1 hour, adding water if necessary. Top with sesame seeds and serve with steamed rice. Sliced fruit, like kiwis or halved green grapes look nice on the plate.

Serves 4

Pink Poulet

2 or 3 pounds chicken pieces

flour

2 Tbsp. cooking oil

2 leeks, sliced (white and light green part only)

1 1/2 tsp. paprika

1/2 cup cranberry sauce

1/2 cup chicken broth

1 Tbsp. wine vinegar

1 tsp. honey or molasses

1 rounded Tbsp. flour

1/2 cup sour cream

salt and pepper

Dust chicken pieces with flour. Brown in oil in heavy skillet. Add leeks and cook 3 minutes more. Mix the paprika, cranberry sauce, chicken broth, vinegar and honey and pour over chicken. Cover and simmer 30 minutes. Mix flour with sour cream and add to chicken. Cook 1 or 2 minutes more, until sauce thickens. Add salt and pepper to taste. I like this served with small boiled red potatoes, but rice or pasta would work just as well. Add a green vegetable for color.

Serves 4 to 6

Magic Maui Burgers

If you're a hamburger lover, this dish is much better than the sum of it's parts.

1/3 pound hamburger per person

jack cheese, sliced

Maui onion, sliced

Maui tomato, sliced

mayonnaise

Magic Maui sauce (page 57)

hamburger buns or sourdough bread

Grill burgers to your taste. Top with a slice of cheese the last 2 or 3 minutes of cooking. Heat buns or bread, sliced. Spread buns lightly with mayonnaise, add a burger, a slice each of tomato and onion and a glob of Magic Maui sauce. Top with the other half of bun and serve.

Hungry Surfers' Stew

This stew is lovely over wild rice with fruit garnish but when the kids come in starving, serve it in scooped out submarine rolls.

1/2 pound Italian sausages (3 or 4 sausages)

2 pounds stewing beef

1/4 cup flour

2 Tbsp. vegetable oil

1 onion, chopped

2 cloves garlic, minced

1 1/4 cups beef bouillon

1/4 cup water

1/2 tsp. salt, few shakes pepper

1 Tbsp. soy sauce

1 Tbsp. Marsala wine

2 Tbsp. hoisin sauce*

Dredge beef in flour. Brown beef and sausage, sliced, in vegetable oil in heavy skillet. Add onions and garlic and cook 2 minutes. Add remaining ingredients and cook slowly 1 1/2 to 2 hours, or until beef is tender. Add water, if needed, during cooking.

* Hoisin sauce is available at Asian markets and many grocery stores.

Serves 4 to 6

Mama Annie's Chicken

This dish has a Southwest flavor so I generally serve it with rice, beans and tortillas. Tutu's tortilla soup would be good with this.

2 pounds chicken, cut in pieces

1 Tbsp. olive oil

1 Tbsp. butter

1 clove garlic

1 onion, sliced

1 8 oz. can tomato juice

1 4 oz. can chopped jalapeno peppers

2 Tbsp. red wine vinegar

1/2 tsp. each, oregano and cumin

1 Tbsp.mild California chili powder

1 tsp. hot chili powder

salt

Wash and dry chicken pieces. Brown in olive oil and butter with garlic and onion. Sprinkle with salt and chili powders. Add tomato juice, jalapeno peppers, vinegar, oregano and cumin. Simmer slowly 40 to 60 minutes.

Serves 4

Piquant Beef on Greens

This is a wonderful hot weather dinner as it is light and fruity but also has a little meat to quench the appetite. This recipe serves 2 but can easily be doubled or tripled.

3/4 pound tender beef, top sirloin, tenderloin or filet

2 Tbsp. orange juice concentrate

2 Tbsp. rice vinegar

2 large cloves garlic, minced

2 heaping Tbsp. minced onion

1 tsp. fresh ginger, minced

3 Tbsp. oil

1 tsp. chopped cilantro

1 tsp. mint sauce

2 cups butter lettuce or mixed greens

1 orange or other fruit for garnish

Combine in a bowl, orange juice concentrate, vinegar, garlic, onion, ginger, oil, cilantro and mint sauce. Put 1/2 of mixture in another bowl. Grill, broil or roast meat until medium rare and slice thin. Arrange lettuce on 2 plates. Toss meat in 1/2 of orange mixture. Arrange slices on lettuce. Drizzle other half of mixture on lettuce leaves and garnish with sliced fruit.

Serves 4

Spicy Chicken Stir Fry

3 chicken breasts, cut in bite-size pieces

2 1/2 Tbsp. cooking oil

cornstarch

1/2 tsp. salt

2 cloves garlic, minced

1 Tbsp. fresh ginger, minced

1 onion cut in narrow wedges

1 green pepper sliced lengthwise

1/4 cup daikon radish, chopped*

2 firm tomatoes, cut in wedges

1/2 cup chicken broth

2 Tbsp. soy sauce

1/2 to 1 tsp. wasabi paste**

Dust chicken pieces with cornstarch and salt. Stir fry in wok or skillet in 1 1/2 Tbsp. oil for 3 or 4 minutes. Remove chicken and add to wok, with 1 more Tbsp. oil, garlic, onion, ginger, green pepper and daikon radish. Cook 3 minutes. Mix chicken broth, soy sauce and wasabi paste and add to wok. Add tomatoes and return chicken and stir just to heat. Serve with rice or in tortillas.

Daikon radish is available in Asian markets and many grocery stores. It looks a little like a large parsnip and tastes like a mild radish.

** *You can buy wasabi paste or buy it powdered and add water to a mustard-like consistency. It's the green horseradish paste served with sushi.*

Serves 4

Hoihoi Pork

Hoihoi means interesting and this dish is. I think you'll find it delicious as well.

2 pounds boneless pork chops

1/4 cup flour

1/2 tsp. each sage and salt

1 Tbsp. oil

1 cup pineapple chunks

1 yam, cubed

1 cup whole berry cranberry sauce

1 Tbsp. orange juice concentrate

1 tsp. honey

1 Tbsp. apple cider vinegar

1 large clove garlic

2 slices fresh ginger

1/2 cup golden raisins

Dredge pork chops with flour mixed with sage and salt. Brown well in oil. Add pineapple and yam and cook 3 or 4 minutes. Mix all the rest of the ingredients together and pour over pork mix. Transfer to oven-proof dish and bake at 325 degrees for 1 hour.

Serves 4

Fish

Curry Coconut Scallops on Rice Cakes

1 pound scallops, shrimp are good too

2 Tbsp. butter

3/4 cup chicken broth

1 1/2 tsp. curry paste, or more to taste

2 Tbsp. peanut butter

3/4 cup coconut milk, canned

2 tsp. corn starch dissolved in 2 tsp. water

salt

2 Tbsp. chopped peanuts or pistachios

Saute scallops or shrimp in butter just until done, 2 or 3 minutes. Remove from pan. Add to pan, chicken broth, curry paste and peanut butter. Stir until combined. Add corn starch mix. Simmer until thickened. Add coconut milk, salt and more curry paste if you like it hotter. Return shellfish to pan and heat through. Serve on rice cakes.

Rice Cakes

1/2 cup sweet rice or short grain rice

3/4 cup water and 1/2 cup coconut milk

2 Tbsp. butter

salt to taste

Cook rice in boiling water and coconut milk until tender but sticky, 15 to 20 minutes. Remove from heat. Add butter and salt. Cool. Form into patties and brown on each side in butter or oil.

Serves 4

Sesame Ahi with Pasta

4 pieces ahi

4 Tbsp. vegetable oil

1 1/2 tsp. sesame oil

1 tsp. honey

1 Tbsp. vinegar

2 cloves garlic, chopped

8 to 10 mushrooms, sliced

1 1/2 tsp. cornstarch

1 cup chicken broth

1 package linguini

2 cups bean sprouts

2 Tbsp. sesame seeds

Combine 3 Tbsp. of the vegetable oil, 1 tsp. sesame oil, the honey and the vinegar and marinate fish in this mixture at least 2 hours or overnight. Saute garlic and mushroom in remaining vegetable and sesame oil. Mix cornstarch with chicken broth and add to pan, stirring to combine and thicken. Remove fish from marinade and add marinade to pan with broth mix. Cook sauce gently, stirring often until mixed, thickened and heated. Broil fish. Cook pasta, adding bean sprouts for the last minute of cooking. Drain pasta and bean sprouts and toss to combine. Add sauce to pasta, toss gently and put on 4 serving plates. Place grilled fish on top of pasta and sprinkle with sesame seeds.

Serves 4

Seafood Coquilles

This is a variation on the classic French dish, Coquilles St. Jacques, which is made with scallops.

2 pounds seafood cut bite-size,
any combination of firm white fish with
shrimp, crab or scallops is good.

4 large green onions, chopped

3 large cloves garlic, minced

3 Tbsp. butter flour

salt and pepper

1 Tbsp. fresh ginger, minced

1/2 cup white wine

1/2 cup mayonnaise (I use low-fat)

salt

Pecorino Romano or any good grated cheese

Saute onions and garlic in half the butter for 2 minutes. Lightly flour and salt and pepper the fish. Add fish, with the rest of the butter, to the onions and brown slightly, 2 or 3 minutes. Add wine and ginger and simmer 2 more minutes until fish is almost cooked through. Remove from heat. Add mayonnaise and more salt if needed. Mound mixture in shells or au gratin dishes and sprinkle cheese on top. Broil 2 minutes until cheese bubbles.

Serves 4

Calamari with Pasta

1 pound calamari rings (can be frozen)

1 egg

1/4 cup milk

1 cup Italian breadcrumbs

1/2 tsp. salt

3 Tbsp. vegetable oil and 3 Tbsp. olive oil

3 cloves garlic, minced

3/4 cup white wine

1 tsp. dried oregano

1 Tbsp. chopped parsley

1/2 to 1 tsp. red chili paste (it's hot!)*

1 Tbsp. butter

1 package penne or rigatoni

2 cloves garlic, minced

1/2 tsp. salt

1 Tbsp. capers

1/4 cup grated Romano cheese

Beat egg lightly with milk. Put 1/2 breadcrumbs and 1/4 tsp. salt in a bag. Dip calamari pieces in egg mixture and transfer, several at a time, to the bag of crumbs. Shake to coat. Repeat until all calamari is coated, changing bag and crumbs half way through. Heat 3 Tbsp. vegetable oil in skillet. Saute calamari and 2 cloves chopped garlic for 5 minutes. Remove calamari and add to pan, wine oregano and parsley. Cook until liquid is reduced by half. Swirl in red chili paste and butter. Return calamari to pan and coat with sauce. Saute 2 cloves minced garlic in remaining olive oil for 2 minutes over low heat. Don't brown. Add salt and capers and toss with cooked pasta. Arrange on plate with calamari. Top with cheese.

Available in Asian markets

Serves 4

Mahi-Mahi on Glazed Onions

4 pieces mahi-mahi

3 sweet onions, Maui or Vidalia

1 Tbsp. oil

2 Tbsp. butter

salt and pepper

1 Tbsp. sugar

1 Tsp. honey mustard

2 Tbsp. water

Thinly slice onions and place them in frypan with 1 Tbsp. oil, 1 Tbsp. butter and the sugar. Cook slowly for 5 minutes, turn them over and cook another 5 minutes until brown and glazed. Stir in mustard and water. Cook 1 minute and set aside. Meanwhile brush fish steaks with butter and salt and pepper and grill. Serve fish on top of a bed of onions.

Serves 4

Sesame-Coconut Crusted Salmon

4 salmon filets

1/2 cup flaked coconut, blended to fine

6 Tbsp. sesame seeds

oil

salt

1/2 cup sour cream

1/2 tsp. chili paste*

2 Tbsp. plum sauce

Spray or brush salmon filets with oil. Combine blended coconut with sesame seeds and coat salmon with mixture. Heat frying pan to medium high and cook salmon 3 to 4 minutes per side or until browned and cooked through. Salt to taste. Combine sour cream, chili paste and plum sauce and serve beside fish. Chili paste is hot so add a little at a time and taste as you go.

Chili paste can be found in Asian markets

Serves 4

Cioppino and Fettuccine

3 Tbsp. olive oil

2 large garlic cloves, minced

1/3 cup diced ham

1 onion, chopped

1 green pepper, chopped

1 16 oz. can chopped tomatoes

2 Tbsp. tomato paste

1 Tbsp. fresh basil, chopped

1/2 tsp. dried oregano

1/4 tsp. fennel seeds, crushed

1 Tbsp. red wine vinegar

1 pound firm white fish, cubed

1 pound medium shrimp

8 clams or mussels

parsley

fettuccine

In heavy saucepan saute onion, garlic, ham and peppers in olive oil for 4 to 5 minutes. Add tomatoes, tomato paste, basil, oregano, fennel seeds and vinegar. Cover, bring to boil, reduce heat and simmer 20 minutes. Clean shellfish and gently lay white fish and shellfish on top of tomato mixture. Simmer 5 to 8 minutes more, until fish is cooked. Discard clams or mussels which haven't opened during cooking. Serve in wide bowls over cooked fettuccine with parsley sprinkled on top. Good with a crusty bread.

Serves 4

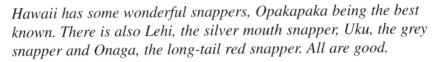

Ratatouille with Snapper

Hawaii has some wonderful snappers, Opakapaka being the best known. There is also Lehi, the silver mouth snapper, Uku, the grey snapper and Onaga, the long-tail red snapper. All are good.

2 Tbsp. olive oil

1 large onion, sliced

2 cloves garlic, minced

2 medium zucchini, chopped

2 Japanese eggplant, chopped

1 green pepper, chopped

2 large tomatoes, chopped

1 cup water

3 Tbsp. tomato paste

1 tsp. dried basil

2 Tbsp. chopped parsley

1 Tbsp. capers

salt

2 pounds fresh snapper

Heat oil in large skillet. Add first 6 ingredients. Stir fry for 5 minutes. Add next 6 ingredients. Simmer, covered, at low heat for 30 minutes, adding a little water if necessary. Taste mixture and add salt to taste. Gently lay fish filets on top of vegetable mixture, cover, and simmer 8 to 10, minutes or until fish flakes easily. Good sprinkled with parmesan cheese.

Serves 4

Ono with Mint Sauce

This is a very simple recipe and very good. Mint sauce is available in all large grocery stores. I use Crosse & Blackwell's.

4 pieces ono

flour

salt

cooking oil and butter

1 1/2 Tbsp. butter

juice of 2 limes

2 or 3 Tbsp. mint sauce

Lightly coat fish with flour and salt. Fry in oil and butter or spray oil, just until done. Remove fish from pan and without washing pan, add 1 1/2 Tbsp. butter, lime juice and mint sauce. Taste as you go as some people like more mint sauce than others. Serve sauce immediately over fish.

Serves 4

Seabass on Blackbeans and Rice

4 pieces sea bass

1 lemon

2 Tbsp. butter

1 1/2 cup cooked black beans

3 cups cooked brown rice

2 Tbsp. white wine vinegar

1/4 tsp. salt

1/2 tsp. cumin

1/2 cup chopped chives

1/4 cup cilantro or parsley

pineapple salsa

Squeeze lemon over fish and dot each piece with butter. Broil fish 10 minutes, or until done. Combine beans, rice, vinegar, salt, cumin and chives and heat in a microwave or oven. Mound beans and rice on four plates, top with fish and surround with pineapple salsa.

Serves 4

Pineapple Salsa (on next page)

Pineapple Salsa

1 cup chopped pineapple
1/3 cup chopped onion
1/2 cup chopped red bell pepper
1 clove garlic, minced
1 tsp. lemon juice
1/2 tsp. sugar
1/2 to 1 tsp. red pepper flakes

Combine all ingredients and allow to sit for a few minutes.

Pasta with Smoked Salmon and Chevre

If you're fond of the taste of smoked salmon and chevre which is a soft goat cheese, you will love this dish. As they are both strong flavors, they are used in moderation.

6 ounces smoked salmon, chopped

1 large clove garlic, chopped

1 Tbsp. olive oil

2 heaping Tbsp. chevre

2 Tbsp. chopped Italian parsley

1 1/2 cups chicken broth

1 Tbsp. pesto*

2 Tbsp. butter

2 Tbsp. flour

1/2 cup milk

2 Tbsp. cream

pasta

Brown garlic in olive oil and remove it. We are just flavoring the oil. Add parsley, pesto and chicken broth. Simmer for 3 minutes. Make a roux by mashing butter into flour. Stir in a little of the hot broth and add mixture to chicken broth mixture, stirring with a whisk to thicken. Add milk, cream and chevre. Stir to heat and add salmon. Stir just to heat and remove from heat. Serve over cooked pasta.

* There is a recipe for pesto on page 17 or you can use a commercial one.

Serves 4

Seared Ahi on Pasta Nicoise

1 1/2 pounds Ahi

freshly ground pepper

cooking oil or spray

1 large onion, chopped

2 cloves garlic, chopped

2 Tbsp. olive oil

4 tomatoes, chopped

2 Tbsp. chopped fresh basil

1 Tbsp. capers, including juice

10 to 12 black olives, oil-cured or kalamata

1 Tbsp. cider or red wine vinegar

salt

4 ounces feta cheese, crumbled

pasta

Buy the ahi in blocks approximately 2"x2". Spray or brush with cooking oil and roll in pepper to coat. Refrigerate. Saute onion and garlic in olive oil, on low heat for about 5 minutes. Add tomatoes, basil, capers, olives and vinegar. Cover and simmer 3 minutes. Add cheese, and salt if necessary. Keep warm. Sear ahi in hot cooking oil turning to brown on all sides. It's very good rare but you can cook it a little longer if you wish, 2 to 3 minutes total for rare and 2 minutes per side for medium. Slice ahi 1/4 inch thick. Serve sauce over cooked pasta with slices of ahi arranged on sauce.

Serves 4

Heavenly Blue Cheese Shrimp

1 1/2 pounds medium shrimp

3/4 cup crumbled blue cheese

3 Tbsp. chopped chives

1 1/2 cups bread crumbs

3 Tbsp. melted butter

1/3 to 1/2 cup dry sherry

1/2 cup heavy cream

Shell and clean shrimp. Blanch in boiling water for 30 seconds. Place blanched shrimp in oven-proof dish or 4 au-gratin dishes. Crumble blue cheese evenly over shrimp. Toss chives and bread-crumbs in melted butter and sprinkle over shrimp and cheese. Drizzle sherry over that and carefully pour cream evenly over all. Cover with foil and bake at 350 degrees for 25 minutes.

Serves 4

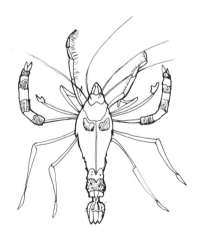

Desserts

Macadamia Coconut Cream

This dessert is rich and delicious. A small portion with fresh fruit on the side finishes a meal beautifully.

1/2 cup shredded coconut

3/4 cup macadamia nuts, chopped

1 1/2 cup milk

1/2 cup sugar

4 egg yolks

1 tsp. vanilla

2 envelopes unflavored gelatin

1 pint heavy cream, whipped

Combine one cup milk with egg yolks, sugar, nuts and coconut. Cook over low heat, stirring constantly, until thick. Remove from heat. Add vanilla. Soak the gelatin in remaining milk. Add a little of the hot mix and stir until gelatin is dissolved. Combine both mixes and cool. When mixture starts to thicken, fold in the whipped cream. Pour into sherbet or dessert dishes and chill.

Serves 4 to 6

Pears Heather

This dessert, as well as being unusual and delicious, is also pretty.

4 fresh pears

2 cups water

1/2 cup sugar

1/2 tsp. vanilla

1 package frozen raspberries

1 tsp. cornstarch

6 oz. cream cheese

milk

1/2 cup walnuts, chopped

Defrost raspberries and add 2 tbsp. sugar. Put in saucepan and set aside. Combine water, remaining sugar and vanilla in another saucepan. Peel and halve pears and simmer, 2 or 3 halves at a time, until just tender, 4 to 5 minutes. Mash cream cheese with a little milk until softened. Mix in chopped nuts. When pears have all cooked and cooled, fill hollow of each one with cream cheese-nut mixture. Put together with the other pear halve and cut large end flat so pear will stand on end. Repeat with other three pears. Chill.

Now make sauce: Mix cornstarch with 2 tbsp. cold water and add to raspberries. Simmer 3 minutes and mash through sieve. Cool. Put one pear on each dessert plate. Pour sauce over and top with nut to garnish.

Celebrity Cheesecake

I call this Celebrity Cheesecake because I am famous among my friends for making great cheesecake. It's so easy, I almost feel guilty.

1 8 oz. package cream cheese

2 eggs

1 cup sugar

1 tsp. pure vanilla

1 small carton sour cream

4 Tbsp. sugar

2 cups graham cracker or cookie crumbs

1/4 cup very soft butter or margarine

1/4 cup brown sugar

Mix crumbs with butter and brown sugar and line the bottom and sides of a springform pan with mixture. Bake 10 minutes at 350 degrees. Cool. Put cheese, eggs, one cup sugar and vanilla in blender. Blend until bubbly. Pour into cooked crust and bake 50 minutes at 350 degrees. Cool. Combine sour cream with 4 Tbsp. sugar. Spread on top of cake and chill for at least two hours.

Serves 6

Variations on Cheesecake

Fruit Topping

fresh fruit of your choice
strawberry glaze

Eliminate sour cream topping. Cut peaches or pears in wedges; apricots, strawberries or grapes in half, and arrange in circles on top of cake. Drizzle entire top of cake with strawberry glaze and chill. The glaze will prevent your fruit from turning brown. You purchase strawberry glaze at most markets, or you can make it by combining one box strawberries, 1/2 cup water, 1/2 cup sugar and 1 tsp. corn starch. Simmer until mushy and strain through a sieve.

Maple Pecan

maple flavoring
1/2 cup pecans or macadamia nuts
1/2 cup brown sugar

Add one teaspoon maple flavoring to cake in place of vanilla. Eliminate sour cream topping. Sprinkle or arrange nuts on top of cake. Put brown sugar and 1/2 cup water in saucepan. Cook until syrupy, 5 minutes or so, stirring frequently. Add 1/2 tsp. maple flavoring. Cool slightly and pour over nuts on cake. Chill.

Lisa's Ono
Banana-Orange Cake

2 cups flour

1 Tbsp. baking powder

1/2 tsp. each, salt and baking soda

3/4 cup sugar

1/2 cup butter

2 eggs

2 mashed bananas (1 cup)

1/3 cup orange juice

1 cup macadamia nuts, chopped

1 tsp. vanilla

Oil and flour a 4 1/2 by 8 inch loaf pan. Preheat oven to 350 degrees. Mix together flour, baking powder, salt, baking soda, sugar and nuts. Melt and cool butter. Beat eggs and mix well with melted butter, orange juice and vanilla. Stir in bananas. Combine egg mixture with dry ingredients and stir just until blended. Bake 45 to 50 minutes, or until toothpick inserted in center comes out clean. Serve warm with whipped cream with a touch of Cointreau or any other orange liqueur mixed in.

Serves 8

Coconut Ricotta Mousse

This dessert is loosely based on an Italian ricotta pudding. It's an eggless mousse, as eating raw eggs is no longer recommended.

1/2 pound ricotta cheese

1/4 cup good quality sweet chocolate, grated

1/4 cup macadamia nuts, coarsely chopped

1/4 cup grated coconut, toasted

1/2 cup whipping cream

2 Tbsp. sugar

1 can litchi nuts

Combine ricotta, chocolate and macadamia nuts. Whip cream, adding sugar as you whip. Fold into cheese mixture. Toast coconut in the oven on a baking sheet for only a minute or two, as it burns easily. Mound ricotta in sherbet or champagne glasses. top with cooled coconut and surround edges with litchi nuts. You can substitute fresh fruit for the litchi nuts if you prefer. Refrigerate until serving.

Serves 4

Bananas Tropicale

4 bananas

1/4 cup butter

1/2 cup each brown sugar and white sugar

1 cup pineapple chunks or mango chunks

1/4 cup peanuts

1/2 cup cream

1 tsp. vanilla

ice cream

Slice bananas in half lengthwise. Place two halves in each of four dessert dishes. Heat butter in saucepan. Add sugar and cook slowly, over low heat, stirring constantly until sugar is dissolved, about 3 minutes or so. Add cream, vanilla and peanuts. Cook 1 minute more. Spoon ice cream onto the banana halves, spoon fruit over the ice cream and pour the warm sauce over all.
Serve at once.

Serves 4

The Bountiful and Beautiful Banana

*The fruit is delectable, the flower bud is eaten as a vegetable,
and the leaves are used to wrap meat, rice and so on for steaming.*

Macadamia Nut Tarts

Crust

1 small package cream cheese

1/4 pound butter

1 cup flour

pinch salt

Cream thoroughly and press into small tart pans, 1 to 1 1/2 inch diameter.

Filling and sauce

1 cup chopped macadamia nuts

3/4 cup brown sugar

1 1/4 tsp. pure vanilla

1 egg, beaten

2 Tbsp. melted butter

powdered sugar

Fill tart pans 3/4 full with nuts. Combine sugar, vanilla, egg and butter. Spoon over nuts, covering them. Bake about 15 minutes at 350 degrees or until bubbly, then about 20 minutes at 250 until crust holds together well. Sprinkle with powdered sugar. These are best made within 2 days of serving.

Makes approximately 1 dozen

Loco-Coco Rice Pudding

2 1/2 cups milk

1 cup coconut milk

2/3 cup raw rice

2 Tbsp. sugar

1/2 tsp. salt

1/2 tsp. almond flavoring, optional

1/4 cup chopped and toasted macadamia nuts

1/4 cup toasted coconut

1 cup heavy cream, whipped

Bring milk and coconut milk to boil in large saucepan. Immediately stir in rice, lower heat and simmer 40 minutes. Remove from heat and add sugar, salt, almond flavoring, nuts and coconut. Chill. Carefully fold in whipped cream and serve.

Serves 6

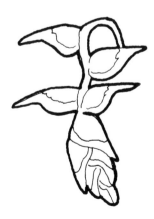

INDEX